7,433,350 7/12
GRUNDY
B/HAN

THAT MAN

'TOMMY'.

THAT MAN

A Memory of
TOMMY HANDLEY
by **BILL GRUNDY**

ELM TREE BOOKS
Hamish Hamilton · London

Other books by Bill Grundy:
Flower of Gloster
All Our Yesterdays
The Press – Inside Out

First published in Great Britain, 1976
by Elm Tree Books Ltd
90 Great Russell Street
London WC1B 3PT

Printed photolitho in Great Britain by
Ebenezer Baylis and Son Limited
The Trinity Press, Worcester, and London

INTRODUCTION

IN HIS DIARIES, published in 1975, that strange man Lord Reith, who created the BBC in his own image, but whose judgment was always suspect, put down the following revealing words:

'30 January, 1949. Wrote to Haley in reply to his of December 28 . . . I permitted myself a cynical PS about the Tommy Handley funeral orgies—roads blocked and the crematorium swamped; a special service in St Paul's conducted by the Bishop of London, and mobs outside. A sociological comment on the age. Dreadful.'

Reith may have written wiser than he knew. It was indeed a sociological comment on the age, if by that he meant it was an accurate indication of how the ordinary people of the time—'mobs', Reith called them—felt about something that had happened on 9 January 1949. And had happened to them.

Because Tommy Handley really did belong to the people in a way that very few other radio entertainers have ever done, and in a way that the aloof Reith never came near to understanding. All through the weary time of war, and the dreary years immediately after, Handley was the voice of the people, or rather, he said the things they would like to have said themselves had they had the wit, the wisdom, or the downright cheek.

The habit of obedience to those set in authority over us was strong in Britain in 1939. It had been induced, to some extent, by the long years of the depression, years when jobs were hard to come by and were therefore not to be thrown away thoughtlessly. For millions, what the boss said, went. They knew, of course, that the boss could be as big a bloody fool as the next man, but it was a brave or foolish fellow who told him so to his face.

Tommy Handley did. As the Minister of Aggravation and Mysteries in the Office of Twerps, as the Mayor of Foaming-at-the-Mouth, as the Governor of Tomtopia, he was an official whose inefficiency was 5

Reith, that stern unbending man

there for all to see. He was Them personified, with all Their faults. But gradually, by one of those processes we kid ourselves is a peculiarly British phenomenon, he came to be the man who was himself official-dom's chief critic. He was the unspoken comment, the insult delivered out of the side of the mouth, the reply other minds may have thought of but few lips dared utter. He was what we would all like to have been.

No wonder Lord Reith, that stern, unbending man who despised almost everybody apart from himself—and especially the ordinary people—felt nothing but contempt for the man who, on the sacred air of Reith's own creation, had actually taught the nation to laugh, not just at itself, but at its masters, too. For Reith, knowing nothing of the people, knew nothing of their idols. Even less did he know why they *were* their idols. Mobs do not have hopes and aspirations: they most certainly do not have a sense of humour. But people do, and understanding people was what Reith was conspicuously bad at and Tommy Handley was conspicuously good at.

Though—or perhaps—because—Reith was a lonely man, he seemed not to feel the need for friendship: indeed, how could he, since he thought most people simply did not measure up to him? But for millions of others, the need for friendship is paramount; and Handley's confident manner, which completely failed to mask his thousand frailties, frailties we all suffer from; and that brisk voice, whose cutting edge could never disguise the friendliness of its owner: these together made up a man who was one of Us, on our side against them.

So when Tommy Handley died on Sunday, 9 January 1949, millions of people really did feel they had lost a friend. The shock was awful. Thursday and Sunday nights would never be the same again. How could they be? We could sit in the same armchair by the fire and switch on the radio at the same time, but the man who had made us laugh, who had lifted our spirits and, in the words of one woman, 'kept us sane all through the war', was gone.

No doubt if Handley had never existed the war would still have been won, and we would still have survived the years after. But the whole of those ten years up to 1949 would have been a lot less endurable, although it is doubtful whether Lord Reith would have understood why, since his gloomy soul could never grasp the healing, even inspiring, nature of laughter. For him, as for the poet Longfellow, life was real, life was earnest: he never seemed to notice that another poet, far more British than Longfellow, spent most of his time praising 'laughter and the love of friends'. Had he done so, he would have realised just why Tommy Handley became so loved in the land, and why his death was such a stunning blow.

It was a blow that left a lasting mark. Even today the *ITMA* catchphrases are part of the language. Even today a letter to the papers about Tommy can bring hundreds of replies—it certainly did in my case. Even today the scripts stand up, particularly if read with memory's ear, so that the old familiar voices are heard in the head. And most of all it is the old familiar voice of Tommy Handley which can bring the past flooding back, and can produce a warm glow, even if that glow is inevitably followed by a feeling a sadness that he, and they, are gone.

Because the memories *do* linger on, because they will be a long time dying, I have written this book. It is, quite simply, an attempt to tell the story of *That Man*.

1

THERE MUST BE something more in the air of Liverpool than the sound of seagulls and ships' sirens. Because that city has surely produced more comedians than any other place of comparable size. Billy Bennett, Robb Wilton, Arthur Askey, Ted Ray, Ken Dodd, Albert Modley (despite his Yorkshire accent), Jimmy Tarbuck, and many others came from, or grew up in, mucky old Merseyside. So when Thomas Reginald Handley was born at 13 Threlfall Street, Toxteth Park, Liverpool, on 17 January 1892, he had quite clearly chosen the right place. Note the date: the reference books all say it was 1894, but the birth certificate in Somerset House indicates that it was two years earlier. Nor was his father, as those same books say, a 'dairy farmer' by profession—surely, an extremely unlikely job for someone living slap-bang in the heart of Victorian Liverpool. John Handley, who died soon after his son arrived on the scene, was a mere 'cow keeper' (which was *not* unlikely, for those were the days when the odd cow or two would be kept in an urban yard to provide halfpenny cans of fresh, if tuberculosis-laden, milk for the neighbourhood).

But however his job is described, John Handley's death presented his young widow with some massive problems. He left no money—he had never had any to leave. And the last years of the Good Old Queen's reign were, in Liverpool as everywhere else, not the best of times for a young uneducated woman to have to scratch out a living and look after a young child at the same time. How Sarah Anne Handley did it we shall never know, because nowhere in the earlier biographies—indeed, not even in Tommy's late 'thirties autobiography *Handley's Pages*—is there a word about what it was like to struggle along on the few shillings a week she was likely to earn as a cleaner or seamstress, the only jobs open to a young woman of her class in the Liverpool of the early 1890s.

Tommy's upbringing, then, is fairly certain to have been poverty-stricken. But the biographies, including even *Handley's Pages*, go out of their way to suggest that at worst it was genteel working-class and at best positively affluent middle-class. At a party, so that Tommy can prepare a trick he has thought up, the other children are asked 'to leave the drawing-room'. It doesn't sound like a Threlfall Street usage: 'parlour', or the straightforward 'front room', seem much more likely. Similarly, after another trick has gone wrong at yet another party, the mother of Tommy's friend writes a note to his mother to tell her that 'the Handley boy need not expect to play with his friend any more'. It doesn't ring very true. She's much more likely to have shouted across the street: 'And I don't want to catch your Tommy playing with our Johnny again.'

The house where this incident is supposed to have happened also sounds improbable in the extreme. Everything in it, 'from carpets to curtain rings', was brand new. I doubt it. Liverpool working-class houses of that time were seldom furnished new from top to bottom; things were bought secondhand or handed down. And if there *were* new things in the house a gang of children would never have been allowed near the place.

These distortions could be put down to the mild fancies of 'ghost writers' (both Ted Kavanagh's 1949 biography and *Handley's Pages* were ghosted), but this may very well give us some clues to the way Tommy was to behave in later life. When he was first trying to make his way on the stage, it was a profession where people took improbably posh names, dressed like aristocrats, and generally behaved as though they had been silver-spooned from birth. Today, actors revel in boasting (perhaps even lying) about their working-class origins. Today, they sometimes go to the trouble of acquiring a working-class accent, even if their own native wood-notes wild were first heard fluting across the lush pastures of Kensington, Chelsea and Knightsbridge.

But not in Tommy's day. Which perhaps helps to explain those mild middle-class improbabilities in which he and his biographers indulged. It may even explain the way John Handley became a 'dairy farmer'; it sounds so much more socially acceptable than 'cow keeper'.

However, whether cow-keeper's kid or dairy-farmer's darling, Tommy Handley was destined to follow a quite different direction. By the age of eight he already possessed a fine, deep, baritone voice, a voice that led to an ambition to become a professional singer. But it also led to the discovery that making people laugh is highly satisfying. And they must have laughed: the combination of a baritone voice and short trousers has just got to be funny.

10   His first stage appearance, aged nine, was in a concert at his

Mrs Handley's Boy

school, St Michael's, Aigburth. It was decisive. From then on, Tommy was bitten by the acting bug. He took up ventriloquism; he practised the art of make-up; he read books with titles like *How to Become an Actor: by A Friend of Sir Henry Irving, Kt.* There was still the hard graft of school work to be got through, but Tommy's thoughts were mostly on the next concert. At Toxteth Congregational Church Sunday school he was able to try out the skills he had been acquiring in a play called *A Bundle of Sticks*, which sounds very reminiscent of the Victorian ballad 'Won't you buy my pretty flowers?', since it concerned the efforts of two little waifs to sell a bundle of sticks to get the price of a loaf of bread. Nobody will buy and the waifs are reduced to shivering tears. Enter Tommy as The Toff, complete with moustache (he loved false moustaches all his life). Instead of offering to buy their bundle, he looked at them and said, without moving his lips, 'I dare you to come to choir practice on Friday in those filthy rags.' Perhaps it wasn't the best ad-lib Tommy ever did in his life, but it was good enough to cause his girlfriend Anne Benson and the other waif to break down into uncontrollable giggles, and the Sunday school teacher to end the performance by hurriedly drawing the curtains.

Choir practice, incidentally, was conducted by his mother's brother, Uncle Will Kelly, and his nephew seldom missed a rehearsal, not because Mother and Uncle insisted on his attendance, but simply because he enjoyed singing so much. Indeed, he sang so splendidly in one famous oratorio that the rest of the choir decided its name ought to be changed to 'Handley's Messiah'. The older members of the choir still called it that as late as the 1930s.

In 1906, when Tommy was fourteen, he left school. In those days most children left much earlier to help the family budget but, despite her straitened circumstances, Mrs Handley had insisted that Tommy stayed on to get as much education as possible: education seemed to

X marks That Man – Llandudno, 1913

her the best way for her son to get on in life and get out of the surroundings in which he had been brought up. All it got him, in fact,
was a job at Riley's wholesale stationers, and then, in 1909, a job selling
prams and other baby necessaries at a shop in Duke Street, just down
the hill from Giles Gilbert Scott's massive (and still uncompleted)
Anglican cathedral. An old wages book shows that he was paid 8s. 6d.
a week, about 43p in our debased modern coinage. Tommy and Anne
Benson used to walk the two miles home each night, he from the shop
and she from a nearby telephone training school, to save the penny
tram fare.

Because he was a bright, personable, young man, never backward at
coming forward, he was soon promoted and his wages went up to 10s.,
or 50p. But though the money was undoubtedly useful at home,
Tommy's heart wasn't really in his work. It was in music and the
stage. He was still an enthusiastic member of the Toxteth choir, under
Uncle Will, and he used to go with them on their annual outings,
usually to Llandudno by steamer from Liverpool Pierhead. It is nice
to think it could have been on one of these outings that Tommy first
saw the famous one-legged 'diver'—nobody ever actually saw him
dive—whose begging cry later became world-famous when it was used
in *ITMA*: 'Don't forget the diver. Every penny makes the water
warmer.'

When he wasn't singing, Tommy was acting. He joined the Aigburth Amateur Dramatic Society, and the Wellesley Society, whose
home was in the famous South Liverpool district of The Dingle, a
name that was to crop up many times in *ITMA* whenever Frisby Dyke
appeared on the scene. He played in *Sweet Lavender*; he was Catter-
mole in *The Private Secretary*; he played the Artful Dodger in *Oliver
Twist*, and he doubled the parts of Bob Cratchit and a deaf old man in
Scrooge. He made a big hit in *Charley's Aunt* and started producing
plays as well. One of them was *The Wrong Flat*, and he was so keen
that, when he found there was a scenery transport problem, he loaded a
handcart with the backdrops and props and pushed it four miles to
where the play was being presented. The play, incidentally, was being
put on for charity, and the charity was to provide knitting wool for
comforts for the Army. Because the year was 1914; the Great War had
broken out; and Tommy Handley's early days were over.

"Maritana"

Sincerely Yours
Tom Harrison
June 1916

2

THE TERRIBLE THINGS happening in Flanders did not interfere very much with the even tenor of Tommy Handley's life. He continued to act whenever and wherever he got the chance. He still went on singing in that fine baritone voice of his, and he was now getting new and useful stage experience. He had joined a concert party that toured forces' camps and canteens in the Liverpool area: playing in all sorts of surroundings and to all sorts of audiences—not just the captive ones of relatives and friends typical of amateur dramatics—was ideal training for what lay ahead. He even appeared in grand opera. It was *Maritana*, by the Irishman W. V. Wallace, which, despite a plot so complicated that it is doubtful if anyone, including the composer, ever understood it, had been a firm favourite with British audiences since its first production back in 1845. Tommy was the King of Spain and quite looked the part (assuming he didn't wear his wrist watch during performances, as he did in the photograph he had taken at the time).

This was 1916, which automatically brings up an odd point. How did it happen that a fit young man of twenty-four, sound in wind and limb, had not volunteered to be slaughtered for King and Country, as so many of his friends had? Why hadn't he been subject to the white-feather treatment so frequently meted out to young men in civvies by ladies who were unlikely in the extreme ever to have to fight in the trenches themselves? And why was it that, though conscription was introduced to Britain in February 1916, Tommy remained a civilian for almost two years after that date? Selling prams in Liverpool, and singing the part of the King of Spain in *Maritana*, can hardly have ranked high on the list of reserved occupations.

No one knows the answers to those questions. Perhaps he saw through the false glamour of the recruiting posters, although in later life he revealed himself as an instinctive conservative patriot, with little or no political insight or understanding. Perhaps the ladies of 15

Liverpool were less aggressive than those in other parts of the country, as well as being used to seeing thousands of men in civilian clothes who were, in fact, serving in the Merchant Navy in a front line every bit as murderous as that in France. Perhaps Tommy wasn't called up simply because of bureaucratic muddle and inefficiency. All we do know is that he didn't join up until November 1917, and the delay gave him the chance to do what his mind had been set on for years— turn professional. In the summer of 1917 he answered a newspaper advertisement for 'a few gentlemen' for a musical comedy, attended an audition at the Royal Court Theatre, Liverpool, and then spent an anxious six weeks before a postcard invited him to present himself at Daly's Theatre. He did so, and found himself a member of the chorus of a touring company of *Maid of the Mountains.*

The tour lasted only eight weeks, covering Scotland and the North of England, but it was enough for Tommy to realise that this was the life. Real actors, real theatres! He revelled in every second of it. The theatrical oyster was about to open at last. Or so it seemed. But things worked out differently. On 11 November 1917, exactly twelve months to the day before war ended, Tommy Handley, actor and singer, late of Liverpool, found himself an airman second-class in the Royal Naval Air Service, signing on in the distinctly un-naval atmosphere of the Crystal Palace in South London. Shortly afterwards he was moved to the equally un-naval atmosphere of Roehampton. But here he was decidedly lucky: if the Roehampton air lacked the smell of ozone, it most certainly didn't lack the smell of grease paint. Within weeks Tommy was a member of a concert party which included no less a person than G. H. Elliott, the Chocolate Coloured Coon. In the eleven months up to the end of the war they staged nearly one thousand shows. They toured in a lorry, giving three or four performances a night at various locations—sometimes on the steps of the plinth of Nelson's Column in Trafalgar Square, sometimes at any old street corner where, competing against the noise of the traffic, they could hope to attract an audience.

They were very much needed. Public morale was low. There seemed no way the war could ever end. The casualty lists were sickening in their size—an average of six weeks' more life was all a soldier could expect once he was sent to the front line. And, in London, Count Zeppelin's great cigar-shaped monsters glittered silver in the search-lights and dropped their load of death on the city beneath. No wonder the concert party was welcomed wherever it went. Music and laughter is a good way to keep sane at a time like that, as *ITMA* was to show, one war later.

It was wonderful training for a comic and by the time the Armistice came along, followed shortly by his demob, Tommy Handley was no longer raw. He was a trouper, able to hold an audience, any audience, he thought, by his line of rapid-fire patter and his ability to ad-lib so well that whatever happened could be turned to advantage.

But the fact was that he actually had very little to offer. He was now twenty-seven but had to his credit only eight weeks of real professional work, and only as a chorus boy in a musical comedy at that. A thousand appearances with G. H. Elliott sounded impressive, but there is a great deal of difference between playing from the back of a lorry or on the steps of Trafalgar Square, and holding an audience in a theatre the size of, say, the Palladium. He had a good singing voice, but it had had absolutely no professional training. Singing in the Toxteth Congregational Church choir was a long way from taking the lead in a West End musical. Making a big hit in *Charley's Aunt* in a Liverpool amateur production was no proof that he could do the same in a professional theatre.

He needed a bit of luck, and he got it. Wandering down Charing Cross Road one day soon after demobilisation, he met a friend he had known in the Royal Naval Air Service who told him there might be an opening with a touring Macdonald and Young show called *Shanghai*. There was, and Tommy got it. Also in the cast was a young pianist called Jackson Hylton. Later on, millions were to know him as bandleader and impresario Jack Hylton. He and Tommy became firm friends. It was a friendship that never stopped working to Tommy's advantage, although at first there was no sign that Hylton was going to shoot so high in the theatrical sky.

Shanghai wasn't very good: it folded in the spring of 1919, and Tommy was back doing the rounds of the agents' offices. But Jack Hylton had been given the job of forming a summer-season concert party at Bognor (not yet dignified by the title 'Regis': George V had not yet gone there to convalesce; nor, therefore, had he died uttering the immortal last words 'Bugger Bognor').

Jack sent for Tommy and offered him the job of second comic. The principal was a comedian the young Handley had much liked when he had seen him in the Isle of Man years earlier. It was soon clear that, although Tommy had nowhere near the experience of old Charles Harvey, he was a far bigger draw. Those months on the back of a lorry were beginning to show their usefulness.

In fact, Tommy was so successful that when the summer season ended, Jack Hylton suggested they go into partnership, with Jack at the piano, Tommy singing, and both of them indulging in a little light

Thomas Handley and Jackson Hylton on their way to fame

comedy. Tommy jumped at the idea and the two young men were over the moon when they were offered a date at the famous Bedford Music Hall in Camden Town, long since destroyed in a cloud of demolition dust. They went down well enough to be offered a £30-a-week booking at a smart café in the West End. This was the life! New dress suits, for in those days every aspiring entertainer had to be properly got-up, white gloves, top hats, brilliantined hair: they fairly glistened as they came on to do their act. But alas for human hopes! They flopped. Café society, busy exchanging the empty banalities of the Bright Young Things, never stopped talking long enough for Hylton and Handley to make an impression. After two weeks they were paid off and they went their separate ways. Tommy was lucky again; within a fortnight he landed a job as lead comic in a burlesque written by Con West and called *Seasoned to Taste*. His number two was an up-and-coming young man named Bobby Howes. It was another useful friendship, for Howes went on to become one of the best-loved light comedians the British stage had known, and his acquaintance with the leading impresarios of the day meant that Tommy always had a voice willing to put in a good word in the right place.

Seasoned to Taste opened at the Metropolitan, Edgware Road, known to every trouper as the Met; now pulled down, it was then the top music hall date. The show wasn't very good. In fact Tommy privately thought it was terrible, but a man must eat. It managed to stagger into the spring of 1920 before it died a well-deserved death.

This time there wasn't another job around the corner. Tommy and a new mate, Sam Cottrell, later to become a theatrical manager, took to hanging around agents' offices, to making a cup of coffee last two hours in the Lyons Corner House in Coventry Street, and to scrounging a meal from Sam's sister when funds had got so low they wouldn't even run to the coffee. One day an agent asked them whether they'd ever worked in films. They both lied manfully and were sent out to a disused gasworks in Hackney, where they were to be paid 15s. (75p) a day for appearing as extras. The film was called *The Laundry Girl* and was produced by a certain Madame Mellor, whose subsequent descent into oblivion was fairly predictable. The company does not seem to have been over-financed: Sam played a butler, but as he had no bow tie, and they didn't have the money to send out and buy one, he had to stand at the back during a fancy-dress party scene and hope nobody would notice that he was improperly dressed. For some mysterious reason, Tommy was a Red Indian. What his performance was like we shall never know, since the film, not surprisingly, was never finished.

After that it was back to Charing Cross Road and cooling cups of coffee with Sam Cottrell and Bobby Howes, ogling the waitresses and throwing lighthearted banter at each other as though they weren't that most abject of objects, the out-of-work actor. But they weren't out of work for long. Sitting 'out front' one day during the summer concert party at Bognor the year before, had been Leslie Henson. He remembered Tommy Handley. On a visit to the Met he had seen him again in *Seasoned to Taste* and liked him even more. He also liked that show's second lead, Bobby Howes, so when he was asked to form a touring concert party for the summer of 1920, he sent for both of them. By this time they were being 'handled' by Norris and Clayton, who can't have done very well out of them, since ten per cent of nothing is . . . nothing. They were therefore only too happy to sub-let Tommy and Bobby to Henson, who guaranteed them forty weeks' pay a year for the next three years. It was a security neither of them had known since they had started in the profession. It was only the bottom rung of the ladder, but at least it looked as though the ladder was resting

Howes (left) *and Handley* (right)

firmly against the wall, and it would require more than an accident to
kick it away.

The concert party was called *The Sparklers*—oh, those 1920s
names—and it played first of all at Llandrindod Wells in mid-Wales,
by no means the nowhere it might sound to those who don't know it.
At that time it was a fashionable spa, a sort of Welsh Bath, with a
flourishing summer season. Tommy Handley, Bobby Howes, and their
leading lady, Doris Townsend, enjoyed themselves enormously and
many years later Tommy was still writing to some of the families he
met there. Fifty-five years on, Stella Pitchford could even remember
the words of Tommy's most successful song. It was called 'Pennsylvania' and went something like this:

> I had a chicken that wouldn't lay.
> I cut its legs off one fine day.

It can't stand up, so IT'S GOT TO LAY.
In Pennsylvania.

They don't write them like that any more.

I suppose it is pointless to ask if Tommy Handley would have been remembered for so long on the strength of those appearances alone—in other words, if he hadn't become famous afterwards? Possibly; but surely only vaguely, with no sharp definition to the memory. Would I, for example, have more than the vaguest recollection of a young comedy duo who were at the bottom of a Phyllis Dixey bill at the Ardwick Hippodrome in Manchester in 1950 if they hadn't gone on to become Morecambe and Wise? No. Even with the benefit of hindsight, those two young men obstinately refuse to be pulled into sharp focus. Similarly, the Tommy Handley whom I saw at a Manchester music hall in the early 1930s is misty, and not just because it is so long ago. He remains misty because at that time he had not become a star. He was an experienced comic, a fine singer, an extremely charming man, well-mannered, and far better dressed than most in a profession that has never been reluctant to wear fine feathers. (Incidentally, were the gentlemanly manners and the impeccable clothes the outward demonstration that he had, as his mother so devoutly wished and worked for, finally left his poverty-stricken childhood behind him? Not necessarily. Other comedians have come from backgrounds as poor, or even poorer, without wanting to demonstrate, by their dress, just how far behind them it all is. But the one thing Tommy's mother always wanted was for her boy to be respectable—a potent Northern working-class word, that!—to be a cut above the others. Which is why he stayed longer at school than they did, why he was always better dressed at school than they were, why he was always freshly washed before he was allowed out to play. The child may be father to man, as the poet assures us; so, in this case, was the mother.)

But for all his talent, for all his experience, for all his good manners and smart appearance, Tommy Handley, at the time of the Llandrindod Wells concert party, was no more than a dependable pro. His personality on stage was warm: it was not compelling. His name was not yet big enough to pull in an audience, even though, once they were in, he certainly knew how to hold them. It was as though he had not yet found the right vehicle, perhaps not even the right medium. But he hadn't long to wait for both to come along and for his career to take off at a speed that was to surprise even him, convinced as he always had been that he was destined for the big time.

TOMMY HANDLEY

0/3839

3

WHEN TOMMY HANDLEY returned to London after the Llandrindod season, Leslie Henson had some news for him. He had come across a sketch he thought would suit Tommy down to the ground. As it happened, Handley had heard it before, because it had been written during the war by Austin Melford and Eric Blore, later to make a name playing the round-faced, sharpish-featured, and very English butler who appeared in so many Hollywood films of the 'thirties.

The sketch was set in an Army orderly room, and featured every traditional Army comedy type, from the gormless private, through the sergeant nobody loves, to the silly ass officer. But it had one feature Henson guessed would really make it work for Handley. All the words were parodies of well-known songs, sung to the appropriate tunes. They ranged from drawing-room ballads to patter songs—the very material Tommy had become so expert at handling over the years. The sketch was, of course, 'The Disorderly Room', perhaps the most famous music hall sketch ever written.

The odd thing is that Tommy didn't think very much of it: at best he thought it would only be moderately received. But from the moment it was introduced into the next Llandrindod Wells season it was a smash hit. He played it at theatres all over the country and wherever he went the houses were packed. From Llandrindod they took it to the Shepherd's Bush Empire, West London. You can judge just how popular the sketch became—without benefit of radio or television, remember—by the fact that at the end of 1923, Tommy Handley and Co. would be summoned by Royal Command to present it before Their Majesties at the London Coliseum. 'The Disorderly Room' sketch began to make Tommy, if not a small fortune, at least a solid income. Every music hall wanted it and since Tommy also did a solo act—both comedy patter and songs—his name was seldom out

The Disorderly Room

of the top billing. In time, as with so many artists who become associated in the public's mind with one particular number, he came to hate the sketch. He tried to drop it from his act, but the Great British Music Hall Audience would have none of it. They wanted nothing else but 'The Disorderly Room'. In true British tradition they liked what they knew they liked.

Also in the true British tradition were the impresarios who thought that if the public had liked Tommy and Co. in one sketch made up of parodies, then they would obviously like them in *another* sketch made up of parodies. They were wrong. 'Wrangle *v.* Wrangle' was a domestic comedy set in a divorce court. It played all the number one halls—the Coliseum, the Alhambra, the Holborn Empire, and so on—but it was never in the same league as its predecessor, with the result that its death at the end of 1922 came as a blessed release.

So back into the repertory, at least for a time, came 'The Disorderly Room'. To relieve the monotony, Tommy used to amuse himself by altering the words of the patter songs, replacing them with gibberish, but gibberish that scanned and rhymed every bit as well as the originals. Phrases like 'the tittifalol bazookas' and 'the skimsons and the skamsons' crept into the songs and soon became part of Tommy's nonsense vocabulary. Without knowing it, he was preparing himself for those glorious bursts of surrealism for which he and *ITMA* were to become famous some twenty years later.

Tommy could see no way of getting on without the sketch. The milestone was showing every sign of becoming a millstone, so he decided to try his hand at something else. He took the job as lead comic in *Dancing Time*, a Levy Bros production which rehearsed for an unprecedented three weeks, a sure sign the management thought they were on to a winner. But from the opening night—at the Penge Empire—it was clear that Tommy wasn't going to make it. He simply didn't yet have the personality, as every 'star' must have, to hold the stage by himself, and lead a big and varied cast. Six weeks later he was given his cards and was replaced by Jimmy Jewell Sr, after which the show ran for the two successful years the management had forecast.

Tommy must have looked after it regretfully and wondered where he himself was going. At first it seemed backwards. It was the old round of 'smokers', Masonics, and concert parties again. He appeared in revue with Nellie Wallace at the Coliseum, and played in pantomime with her. Then into a Palladium revue, *The Whirl of the World*, with Nellie again, Billy Merson, and Nervo and Knox, later to become part of the famous Crazy Gang. His name was being seen in the lights of the West End, but never as lead. The lack of star quality was still obvious. As a member of a team Tommy had few equals. As a solo spot he simply wasn't in the top class, not even after 'The Disorderly Room' had been featured in the 1923 Royal Command Variety Performance.

But in one way that 'Royal' was a turning point. The year before, a long, gaunt, young, Scottish engineer had been appointed general manager of the newly-formed British Broadcasting Company. His name was John Reith, the same John Reith who, twenty-seven years later, ennobled but embittered, was to express in his diary such scorn for the crowds who turned up at the Handley memorial services. But back in 1922 he was merely a God-driven Scotsman on the make, whose brief was to set up a British radio service. By March 1923, when there were still only about 30,000 licence holders in the country, the BBC (still Company, not Corporation) had moved to Savoy Hill, lying between the Strand and the River Thames. And in December 1923 it relayed, for the first time ever, a Royal Command Variety Performance. One of the items broadcast was 'The Disorderly Room'. Tommy Handley had spoken, or rather sung, his very first words over the air.

And then . . . nothing. Just a feeling of anti-climax. The old round of agents' offices; the old round of music halls and clubs; but this time with a curious feeling that what they were doing down at Savoy Hill might be the way things were going to go. And then one day he bumped into Jimmy Lester, who had produced the *Dancing Time* revue in which Tommy had been such a flop. Despite that failure, Jimmy had always found something immensely attractive about Tommy's breezy manner, his speed with a script, and the unmistakable cutting edge of his voice. Now producing for the BBC, Lester asked Tommy if he'd care to come along for an audition. The very fact that it was Lester, the producer of Tommy's biggest failure, who was inviting him, made him chary of accepting the invitation. But Lester persisted and so he went. He was an immediate success. At the very moment, therefore, that *Dancing Time* was coming to the end of its run, the comic who hadn't been good enough for it was making his first mark on the airwaves, and making his mark with such mastery that those who heard him knew that Thomas Reginald Handley, comedian and singer, had found absolutely the right medium for himself at last.

Early days at Savoy Hill. Handley with Heather (Thatcher) and, overleaf, with cast of 'How's That' revue

4

THE DISCOVERY CAME just in time. Despite the periods of unemployment and the shock of being fired from *Dancing Time*, Tommy, as some of his friends found out, had begun to develop a bit of a big head. People who worked with him found their names appearing in ever-smaller print on 'The Disorderly Room' posters. Old friends visiting the stage door found messages that said 'Mr Handley is too busy to see you'. That may have been true, but it was none the less unpleasant, and was very unlike the Tommy of old.

'The wireless' saved him. Even if a medium is an artist's *true* medium, it still requires hard work before it is completely mastered. Those early broadcasts from Savoy Hill taught Tommy that, however much he thought he knew about the stage, here was one side of the business he knew absolutely nothing about. He needed to work at it if he was ever going to conquer it. Well, conquer it he did. But in doing so he learned something else. He learned a humility and a faculty for self-criticism which was never to desert him again. Oddly enough, radio taught him self-doubt, too. By one of those paradoxes that make life what it is, the more he succeeded in his new career, the more uncertain he became, the more sure that disaster was always just around the corner. Proof of this is that, even as his BBC reputation grew, he fell back on the assured success of 'The Disorderly Room', the very sketch he had become so bored with the year before. He played it regularly, at theatres all over the country, until 1938. In retrospect it seems absurd: a knockabout comedy of life in the Great War trenches still topping the bill after Hitler had annexed Austria, had occupied Czechoslovakia, and was preparing his Stuka dive-bombers for the destruction of Poland! Outdated it may have been: the important point was that it was a wage-packet, a lifebelt that Tommy was not going to throw away until he was sure he could float without it. And so, though his BBC broadcasts were making him a

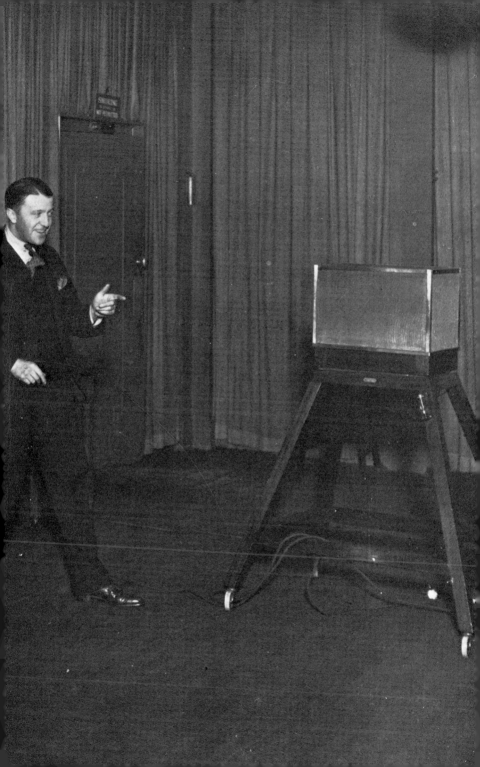

household name, though offers to advertise all sorts of goods and open all sorts of shops, stores, fêtes and functions, came pouring in, Tommy Handley still dragged his company round the halls, flogging as much life, for as long as he could, from the dead horse of 'The Disorderly Room'.

In any case, he needed the money. He was soon to find out that there is no truth in the old saying that two can live as cheaply as one. At Savoy Hill, in 1925, he had worked with a young singer called Jean Allistone. The series, long since forgotten, though hailed as a little masterpiece at the time, was called *Radio Radiance*. Tommy and Jean hit it off at once. She was divorced, he was single. He was beginning to believe at last that the work might keep coming in. There was something about the Handley voice, and the Handley manner, that suited the microphone particularly well. The man who hadn't had the personality to hold the stage in *Dancing Time* was beginning to show that he now had enough personality to hold an audience which, by the late 1920s, was numbered in millions. And even if things went terribly wrong with radio, there was still the security of his music

32 hall work. So he plucked up his courage and married Jean in 1929.

It was the best thing he could have done. Despite her own stage fame—she had played leads for impresarios of the day like Firth Shepherd, Wylie and Tate—she retired from the profession, content from then on to be Tommy's wife, his help-meet, his constant but constructive critic, and his comfort when the notices weren't quite as friendly as they might have been. For Tommy, despite that extrovert manner, was abnormally sensitive to hostile criticism. Indeed, as we shall see, it could be said that he was to prove fatally sensitive to it.

But by the late 1920s there was very little criticism of any kind. After the success of *Radio Radiance*, he appeared in several other series, many of them specially written for him, as their titles show—*Handley's Manoeuvres* and *Tommy's Tours* were just two of them. And increasing radio fame meant increasing pull in the music hall. People who had heard his cheery voice on the wireless were only too keen to leave their firesides and pay good money to see him in the flesh. The bookings poured in and so did the money. But Tommy and Jean lived quietly: the old insecurity was still there. Indeed, Gordon Kay, who helped Ted Kavanagh to write the posthumous biography of Tommy rushed out in the spring of 1949, says that as late as the mid-1930s they were still living in 'a rather tatty flat on the first floor of a house near Paddington Station'. Tommy never thought of buying

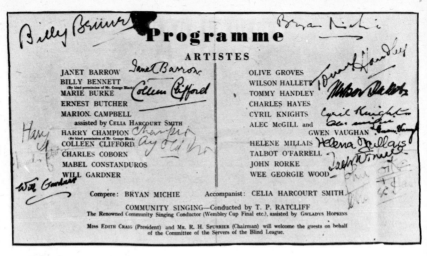

Look at the cast list!

a big car—indeed, he never possessed one in his life. And he never thought of living it up on tour. Every town had its 'pro' pub where the artists playing that town used to gather around lunchtime for a drink and a gossip. Tommy was rarely, if ever, seen there. Hard-earned money had to be put by for a rainy day, not poured down the throats of thirsty colleagues. Like so many comics, Handley, despite the breezy, devil-may-care nature of his act, was always 'careful'.

But he was never stand-offish. Any theatrical landlady who had ever put Tommy up would vouch for that. Letters in that beautiful handwriting of his would constantly be dropping through their letter boxes. Any autograph hunters at the stage door would be asked if they'd like to see the show, and free tickets would be arranged. Anybody who sent him an idea for a gag would be sure of a payment for it: 'I don't work for nothing,' he would say. 'Why should you?' The ladies of the chorus would receive a bottle of sherry each Friday night 'With the compliments of Mr Handley'. Not much perhaps, but it showed kindness. Tommy Handley may have been careful: he was never mean.

All through the 'thirties he prospered. As well as his 'home' radio shows, he did *Handley's Half Hour*, written by Rex Diamond, for the overseas service. And his stage commitments continued to increase too. There was scarcely a music hall in the land he didn't play. Nor a cinema, either, for those were the days when a night at the movies meant a feature film, a B film, a newsreel, and a stage act! The strain must have been tremendous but Tommy seemed to thrive on it.

34

'I can sleep anywhere,' he used to say. And he needed to: he frequently travelled more than 1500 miles a week, largely by rail, and often including a couple of nights on the sleeper. It didn't seem to do him any harm, but hindsight says it also didn't do him any good. The hypertension which in the end brought about his fatal cerebral haemorrhage must have started developing round about now. But Tommy didn't know, and, not knowing, didn't care. So he didn't let up. And how could he? For in the mid-1930s he teamed up permanently with a man he'd already worked a few shows with, Ronald Frankau. The combination of Liverpool-born slum boy and Old Etonian son of a City cigar merchant seemed an unlikely recipe for success. But it worked, and Tommy and Ronald went on to become possibly the most famous of the pre-war radio double acts, Murgatroyd and Winterbottom, an act whose rapid-fire patter style seems, on looking back, to have been the final stage of Tommy Handley's apprenticeship, the last stretch of that long road that was to end with *ITMA*.

5

THE THING THAT was different about Murgatroyd and Winterbottom was their speed. All the other acts of the time, such as Clapham and Dwyer, Bennett and Williams, Robb Wilton, Sandy Powell, Stainless Stephen (who even spelt out the punctuation in his sentences!), all had their own leisurely quality. Murgatroyd and Winterbottom had none. They were sheer speed. If we didn't get the joke, hard luck. If we missed the next three wondering about the first one, harder luck still. But, in time, they taught us to keep up with them. The big problem was laughter. We were in a constant dilemma: should we let go and really enjoy that one, or should we keep everything more or less bottled up until the satisfying release of the final burst of applause? It was a problem Murgatroyd and Winterbottom never appeared to have thought about. They just raced along and left us to work it out for ourselves.

In fact, of course, they *had* considered the problem, and a study of their scripts shows just how they solved it. A typical act would contain splendid puns (if such there be), awful puns, and frankly feeble puns, as well as good gags, moderate gags, and gags that should never have been born. But delivered at such a speed, we never had time to notice the weaknesses. The gag that would have produced an embarrassed half-titter if they'd waited for a reaction simply disappeared without trace, and the half-titter it *might* have produced somehow found itself part of, and thereby increasing, the next laugh.

The other way in which they differed from most double acts of those days is that neither of them was the 'straight' man. Each was the comic, each capped the other, and each joke derived from the last one. It was stream-of-consciousness stuff and it led them down some very odd paths:

Murgatroyd: *How are you, Mr Winterbottom?*
Winterbottom: *I feel a bit funny.*
M: *Only a bit? I feel frightfully funny.*
W: *Well, it ought to be a good act tonight.*
M: *It won't be appreciated by the studio audience.*
W: *Why not?*
M: *Well, look at them—there's a fellow there eating cheese.*
W: *Yes, he got in on the strength of that. They certainly don't look a very intelligent lot.*
M: *No. Obviously friends of the producer's. But we must think of the listener.*
W: *I am thinking of her. There won't half be a row when I get home.*
M: *Why?*
W: *I threw a shoe at her.*
M: *It isn't June yet.*
W: *What's that got to do with it?*
M: *Ne'er cast a clout till May is out. Yes, Mr Winterbottom, we must always study the listener—the Mr and Mrs Everyman.*
W: *The Jones and Smiths.*
M: *The Robinsons and Browns.*
W: *The Gilberts and Sullivans.*
M: *The Tristans and Isoldes.*
W: *The Hengists and Horsas.*
M: *The Moodies and Sankeys.*
W: *And the Derbys and Joans.*
M: *Cut out the Joans and let's think of the Derby. What have you backed?*
W: *My car into a shop window. Joan a car?*
M: *Cut out the Joan and let's think of the Derby again.*

Which they did, with an advance commentary on the Derby which was due to be run the following Wednesday. In other words, from a friendly opening greeting, they passed, by way of insulting the audience and then the producer, through a list of all the double acts you are unlikely ever to meet, and had started a commentary on a race that hadn't yet been run, and all in fifty seconds, with every link a logical one!

Now nobody would claim that the script—*on paper*—looked a riot. But delivered in their own rapid-fire manner, it brought the house down. And it went on for another eight minutes or so, getting wilder and wilder, more and more Goon-like, each second. On the way, they named every single horse in the race, mentioned several of the jockeys,

did seven impersonations of currently-popular music hall acts, incorporated a parody of 'The Charge of The Light Brigade', and tipped no less than twelve winners, as well as going very near the knuckle with this tongue-twister:

W: *What are they waiting for?*
M: *The shostel pit.*
W: *The shistol pot.*
M: *The postel shut.*
W: *The gun!*

The sigh of relief as they got that right, and at high speed too, was almost audible. I shudder to think what an uproar there would have been if that one missing mix-up of vowels had slipped out across the still very much Reith-dominated air, at a time when even saying 'Damn' was thought a suitable case for treatment with something like the death penalty.

The abiding memory of Handley's delivery of such ultra-rapid lines—he was Winterbottom, by the way, but it never seemed to matter as neither of them, as has already been noticed, was the straight man—is that every single word was clearly heard: the diction was now well-nigh perfect. The Liverpool accent of his early days had gone, but he had retained his typically Northern attack on vowels and consonants. The result was a voice and a technique that was ideal for radio. Coupled with all that experience on the halls, coping with every possible type and size of audience, it was obvious that Tommy Handley was cut out to be radio's first really big star.

And yet . . . a star is someone whose name alone will bring the crowds flocking in, or have them rushing home to start twiddling the wireless knobs like mad so as not to miss anything of the act. Tommy had not yet quite achieved that. All his successes had been in the company of others, but not as solo star plus supporting cast: merely as *primus inter pares*, first among equals. Even those shows which featured his name in the title, such as *Handley's Half Hour*, *Handley's Manoeuvres*, and so on, were not really his programmes. They were more like potted versions of the revues so popular on the stage, with Tommy as lead comic, and perhaps singing a song or two. In no sense were they star vehicles: they couldn't be, because, despite everything, Tommy was not yet a star.

Well, why not? That was a question he must have asked himself a thousand times. How much more experience did he have to have? It was also a question BBC producers were beginning to ask. Here is a man who can do anything in front of a mike; who is the life and soul of the party, even a party of his fellow pros; who has played just about every date in the country; so why isn't he up there in the big star bracket?

It began to dawn on the BBC hierarchy that perhaps they were to blame, perhaps they hadn't yet come up with the right vehicle. Which is why, all through 1938, there was a series of meetings at Broadcasting House, into which the Corporation had moved from Savoy Hill in 1932. The theme was—what shall we do with Handley?

Three very experienced 'Variety' men—as the Light Entertainment department was then called—got together and listened to as much American radio material as was available to them, and ultimately came up with an answer which, in view of their experience, was just about as wrong as it could be. The wise men were Eric Maschwitz, former Head of Variety; Charles Brewer, who had been his first lieutenant; and John Watt, who had succeeded them. All three were friends and admirers of Tommy and had helped and encouraged him throughout his broadcasting career. That they proposed something so totally inappropriate goes a long way to proving the truth of the old saying about where a road paved with good intentions leads to.

They came up with the idea of a show which would be based on the

George Burns and Gracie Allen programme, currently the rage of the American radio networks. Even at first glance it was an ill-conceived notion. George Burns was almost silent throughout his act, leaving the non-stop, zany, and very funny gabble to his partner Gracie. To suggest that this would be a suitable vehicle for making a star out of a man who had long shown he was Britain's best fast-talking comedian seemed almost deliberately perverse. It wasn't, of course. It merely showed the domination which American radio, using all those famous Hollywood names, had achieved over the thinking of the British entertainment industry.

Tommy was unhappy with the idea from the first. The scripts weren't all that bad, but they just weren't him. So he went on with his other radio series; he toured the halls—with 'The Disorderly Room', of course; he did special concerts, including one in which he shared the bill with Harry Champion and Charles Coburn, direct links with the great tradition of the music hall which, ironically, Tommy and others were in the process of destroying by means of the top-class entertainment the radio was introducing into almost every house in the country. He did newspaper ads, including one which showed him recommending a new type of motor-car suspension, a subject about which he knew precisely nothing; he made advertising films, including one about power laundries, which had not been released when war broke out, and mercifully never was.

The planners came up with nothing. As the European political climate darkened, as war grew ever more likely, Tommy went on with his work of making people laugh, largely unaware of what was going on in world politics, and hoping against hope that soon someone would come up with the big one he felt was now about due to him. He himself had little idea what form it might take: he was never much of an originator—his were the skills of the performer, the interpreter. And while he hoped, the BBC had another think. They appointed a new producer and a new scriptwriter, both of whom had worked with Handley before, but never on a regular basis.

One sunny afternoon in June 1939, three men sat down in the lounge of the Langham Hotel, just across Portland Place from the BBC, and, ordering gin and tonics, got out pencils and paper and started talking. As it happened, they were surrounded by a convention of clergymen taking tea and scones. Whether the visiting clergymen eavesdropped on their lay neighbours is unknown. If they didn't, they missed something. For the three men were Tommy Handley, comic; Ted Kavanagh, scriptwriter; and Francis Worsley, producer. *ITMA* was about to be born.

The three wise ITMA monkeys. Hear all, write all, say all. Producer Francis Worsley, script-writer Ted Kavanagh and That Man

6

THE PREVAILING IDEA that *ITMA* was a smash hit from the word 'Go' couldn't be more wrong. It wasn't even called *ITMA* at the beginning. The title was actually *It's That Man Again*, a phrase the *Daily Express* had started to use in its headlines whenever Adolf Hitler made yet another 'final territorial demand'. The contraction to the famous initials only came two or three months later, as Tommy was doodling on his note-pad at a script conference.

The first show was transmitted from the BBC's Maida Vale studio on Wednesday, 12 July 1939. It ran for forty-five minutes, from 8.15 to 9.00 pm, and was introduced by the celebrated signature tune which Michael North had written specially for the programme. The band was the Jack Harris Orchestra from the London Casino. The signature tune, and Handley's unmistakable voice, were just about the only resemblance to the show it was later to become. There were several feature items included in the script, with the result that it was not very different from the sort of radio revues Tommy Handley had been doing for years. But there was a 'situation' element: the show was set on board ship. Tommy was the entertainments officer, assisted by a dumb blonde secretary, naturally called Cilly, and hampered by Vladivostooge, a mad Russian inventor. Canadian actress Celia Eddy played Cilly; the Russian was played by Eric Egan.

Though there was the usual atmosphere of 'You were marvellous, darling' after the show, nobody connected with that first transmission was really very impressed in the cold light of the next morning. But it was scheduled to run fortnightly, so run fortnightly it did, at least until the Radiolympia show started on 23 August. It was due to re-start a limited run on 5 September, but that was one date the *ITMA* team didn't keep. On 1 September Hitler invaded Poland, and on 3 September we were at war.

It had, of course, been as obvious to the BBC as it had been to millions of others, during that jittery summer of 1939, that war was becoming more and more inevitable. Contingency plans had therefore been drawn up for the event. They involved a massive dispersal of broadcasting staff, for Stanley Baldwin's remark that the bomber will always get through was very much in people's minds. Everyone expected the declaration of war to be followed by a huge wave of aerial attacks. In the event, of course, nothing happened as far as Britain was concerned. The British Expeditionary Force moved over to France without a single casualty and, when it got there, found there was no fighting for it to do. For this was the period of 'The Phoney War', as one American commentator dubbed it, a name that stuck.

But no one was to know that at the time, of course, so the contingency plans were duly put into effect. The signal was to be a change of phrase in introducing the news. Instead of 'This is the National Programme', the announcer would say 'This is London' and everybody within the BBC would know that the balloon was going up. Tommy Handley, in common with many other key figures, had long known the code signal, so as soon as he heard the words he packed his bags and left for Bristol.

It was the beginning of a tremendously hectic period for him. For a fortnight or more the nation's entire broadcasting output seemed to consist of Tommy in revues and sketches of one kind or another, with musical interludes supplied by Sandy Macpherson at the theatre organ. Ted Kavanagh, the *ITMA* scriptwriter, had also turned up in Bristol, but there was no hope of reviving the show for the delightfully insane reason that, somehow, producer Francis Worsley, who lived in a tiny village miles from London, had never been told of the warning code words. It was some days later that he wondered where all his mates had got to, tracked them down, and then found that all trains to the West Country had been commandeered for troop transport and for evacuating children to the countryside. Then, miracle! A taxi appeared from nowhere. Worsley loaded his family and his luggage into it, and drove all the way to Bristol in style, and at the sort of cost that created havoc in the accounts department when he finally submitted his expenses.

Considering the chaos caused by the descent of hundreds of actors, musicians and administrators on Bristol's comparatively small Broadcasting House in Whiteladies Road, it is remarkable that Francis Worsley was able to produce the first wartime *ITMA* on Tuesday, 19 September, only sixteen days after the declaration. It was even more remarkable when one considers that Worsley's original cast members were not available to him, as they hadn't been vetted by the Security

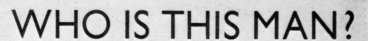

WHO IS THIS MAN?
(WHO LOOKS LIKE CHARLIE CHAPLIN)

Words and Music
by
JOHN WATT and
MAX KESTER.

FEATURED, BROADCAST & RECORDED BY
TOMMY HANDLEY

33, SOHO SQUARE. W.1.

6D.

people. Neither had Ted Kavanagh, by the way, but 'an arrangement was come to', and so the three of them could get down to work. They had plenty to work with, for the new cast included such soon-to-be-famous names as Jack Train, Maurice Denham, Sam Costa, Vera Lennox and—an echo of Tommy's early days—Jack Hylton's Band, although Jack had by now handed the baton over to Billy Ternent.

The first of the wartime shows was given in the Clifton Parish Hall in front of a small invited audience from 9.30 to 10.00 pm. It is doubtful if any of those present that night had the faintest idea that they

were in at the birth of one of the most famous radio series ever. But it is quite certain that within seconds the style was established. Tommy came on and rattled off the following words: 'Heil folks! It's Mein Kampf again! Sorry! I should say: Hello folks! It's That Man Again! That was a Goebbled version a bit doctored. I usually go all goosey when I can't follow my proper-gander.' Then the telephone rang and Tommy found himself engaged in one of those mad conversations which became so much a part of the show. And after that . . . The Door opened. That famous *ITMA* door! Its sole purpose was to bring in the procession of lunatics who were constantly stopping Tommy getting on with his job. But, in the mysterious way that imagination works, the door immediately assumed a personality of its own. No cast list would have been complete without it. And always *two* rattles of the handle before it opened!

'Stopping Tommy getting on with his job.' Yes, but what *was* his job? Even with the benefit of the scripts it is hard to say. Theoretically, he was a Cabinet Minister—the Minister of Aggravations and Mysteries, at the Office of Twerps. But what did he actually do? He tried to cope with his staff and the constant interruptions, is about the only answer one can come up with. Cilly, his first secretary, had been replaced by her sister Dotty, played by Vera Lennox; the mad Russian inventor was still there, for some reason, but his name had now changed to Vodkin, and the role had been taken over by Maurice Denham. Mrs Tickle, the office char who always did 'my best for all my gentlemen', precursor of Mrs 'Can-I-do-yer-now, sir?' Mopp, appeared on the scene, also played by Maurice Denham. And, of course, there was Jack Train. At first Jack was a civil servant, Fusspot, always outraged by Tommy's suggestions—'It's most irregular, *most* irregular'—but he had an enormous range of voices so that at any moment he could be Fusspot, Farmer Jollop, a miscellaneous range of men who rarely said anything other than 'Oomph', and of course, Funf, the totally incompetent but impossibly persistent German spy, who seemed to be in the know about whatever Tommy was doing, but never seemed to be able to do anything to stop it, apart from making threatening noises down the telephone. Those sepulchral tones, by the way, were produced by Jack holding a glass tumbler sideways on to the microphone and speaking into it. It is a measure of the show's success that within weeks of Funf's first appearance—in the second show, on 26 September—you could barely pick a phone up throughout the length and breadth of the land without somebody introducing themselves with 'This is Funf speaking'.

Funf is a perfect example of how *ITMA*, though surreal to the point of insanity, invariably was inspired by real life. For those early days of war, when nobody had any idea what was going on, when the black-out was a troublesome novelty, and a curtain not properly closed could mean that the occupant of the house was signalling to the enemy—those early days and nights produced a lot of over-reaction. Funf helped to smooth away the half-buried fears most people had, fears of an enemy just across the North Sea, whose armed forces had already shown in Poland just how destructive and apparently irresistible they were. As so often with the British, laughter helped us maintain a sense of proportion. The whole of *ITMA*, of course, with its constant satire on bureaucracy, on the idiocies of the time, and on all the difficulties we had to put up with, helped to maintain that sense of proportion: Funf was merely the first of the mad band of characters who helped to keep us sane.

It took just two shows to make Funf a national institution. It took just three to get rid of an entirely extraneous quiz spot, and replace it with a spoof commercial radio station: '*Ici Radio Fakenburg. Défense de cracher!*' and the famous signing-off slogan: '*Mesdames et Messieurs, vous pouvez cracher!*' And it took no more than six weeks for *ITMA* catchphrases to be heard everywhere. The show was clearly a winner. Why? Obviously because of the sheer high spirits of the scripts; obviously because of the enormous gallery of characters; obviously because of the ridiculing of all the bureaucratic idiocies of the times. But most obviously because of Tommy Handley. He kept the show tightly pulled together. He was never crushed by the indignities thrust upon him. He was never downhearted. That cheery voice, rattling out its nonsense, its digs at officialdom, radiated a marvellous heart-warming confidence. We had no idea what lay ahead for us, but insofar as Tommy *was* us, we knew we wouldn't go under. And those who had watched Tommy's career through the years began to realise that, on his own personal level, he had made it at last. He was no longer just a solid, dependable pro. He had finally, even though belatedly, become a star.

Previous pages: *Two very wrong numbers! Jack (Funf) Train*, left *and Dino (So-So) Galvani*, right

7

THAT FIRST WARTIME series, though clearly a success, was only a short one. It ended in February 1940. There were two reasons for this. The decision had been made to evacuate the Office of Twerps to the safety of the seaside (this was still some months before the big air-raids started, so it was an almost psychic piece of foresight), which meant a lot of re-thinking. The second reason, which indicates what a winner the show had already become, was that Tommy's old friend Jack Hylton had decided to mount a stage version of *ITMA*. He took Tommy, of course, Jack Train (equally of course), and Maurice Denham. They opened on 26 February, at the Birmingham Hippodrome, and went on to tour the country for six months.

In terms of seats sold, the tour was undoubtedly a success. Everybody seemed willing to pay money to go and see the men behind the voices, even though it meant going out into the black-out, with the inevitable torch with tissue paper over the lens as the only light, and coping with all the difficulties of severely reduced public transport services, or driving a car with masked headlights, with all the danger *that* involved. But although Jack Hylton got his money back—no mean feat in those circumstances, since it was a lavish and expensive production—the show could not be said to have been an artistic triumph. For the truth was, as should have been obvious to old campaigners like Hylton and Handley, that *ITMA* was purely a radio show. It worked through the imagination; each listener sitting facing his set (those were the days before transistors: a radio was a substantial piece of furniture, so families naturally sat grouped around it as they listened) could supply the voices with whatever form and face he fancied. That indispensable door had a life of its own on the radio: in a theatre it was simply a door.

Nevertheless, Jack Hylton made plans for a second season, but this time on a much less lavish scale. And at a time when high explosive and

That Man with John Watt

incendiary bombs were raining down on our towns and cities, for the Phoney War had exploded into violent life in the late spring of 1940, Tommy Handley was persuaded to revive that old First World War stand-by, 'The Disorderly Room', as part of the show!

All this meant that the return of the radio series had to be postponed. In any case, it would have been extremely difficult to broadcast it from Bristol again. For the Blitz was now hitting all the major cities, not just London, and Bristol was very much in the firing line, with oil depots and Filton airfield so near. Studios were damaged, and soundproofing was destroyed, so that sound effects were quite often much more contemporary than the hard-pressed producers could have wished for! In the end it became too much. The BBC considered all its options and, in February 1941, decided to move lock, stock, and barrel from Bristol to Bangor in North Wales. It was an amazing piece of organisation, when all those wartime difficulties are taken into account, and there don't seem to have been any casualties. Everybody was loaded on to a special train in Bristol, with their wives, children, prams, bikes, pets—one man even tried to put a horse into the guard's van—and many hours later, tired, hungry, but safe, they arrived in Bangor.

One of the people who had gone ahead of that strange caravan was scriptwriter Ted Kavanagh, so it was natural that, as soon as they had all settled in, Francis Worsley and he should start thinking of a new *ITMA* series. Tommy was still on tour, but was expected to be free by the late spring or the early summer. They decided to let him run for election as Mayor of a perfectly horrible seaside resort called Foaming-at-the-Mouth. The termination of Tommy's Cabinet Ministry was lightly skated over; he was duly elected, and the second wartime series started at 8.30 pm on Friday, 20 June, with the new title *ITSA— It's That Sand Again.*

It was now nearly eighteen months since the show had gone off the air. Yet such had been its impact in the first short run that few addicts of the programme can believe it was ever off the air for so long, and through one of the darkest periods of the war at that. So much had *ITMA* and Tommy, like Arnold Bennett's Denry Machin, The Card, become identified with the great cause of cheering us all up that, seen down the wrong end of the telescope of time, the gap between the two series seems minimal, if not actually non-existent.

The lay-off had not harmed the show. Indeed, it seemed to improve it. This short summer season, from June to July 1941, followed by a long season starting in September, was absolutely vintage stuff. It is

Williams of Bennett and Williams v. *Handley of* ITMA. *Loser – the game of golf*

from this time that some of the most famous *ITMA* characters date. Of the original cast only Jack Train and Vera Lennox survived. Many, like Maurice Denham and Sam Costa, had gone into the Forces. Once again Kavanagh and Worsley had to start almost from scratch. But what a team they assembled! Horace Percival as Ali Oop the seller of saucy postcards—'Very chummy. Oh lumme'; Sydney Keith as Sam Scram—'Bawss, bawss, sumpn terrible's happened'; Jack Train's absolutely unintelligible Jap; those genteel handymen Claude and Cecil—'After you Claude.' 'No. After *you* Cecil'; and dozens more. Clarence Wright's ludicrously optimistic salesman—'Good morning. Nice day'—who never actually succeeded in selling anybody anything; Dino Galvani's Signor So-So, endlessly murdering the English language—'Ah, Meestair Handlebar, I am diluted. Let me kick your hand'; Sam Scram's American relative, Lefty, the gangster with the shakes—'It's my noives, I tell ya, it's my noives'; all these date from the 1941 seasons. As well as perhaps the greatest char of all time, Dorothy Summers' gravel-voiced Mrs Mopp, always asking if she could dust the dado or some such, but always preceded by that superbly strident greeting 'Can I do yer now, sir?'

It is interesting to note the Kavanagh didn't get her famous phrase right at first. What he actually wrote for Dorothy Summers was 'Can I do for you now, sir?', and it stayed that way for some weeks until, quite by accident, she misread the script, missed out the word 'for', and the phrase was suddenly there, obviously *exactly* what Mrs Mopp would say.

By now there was such an enormous list of characters, past and present, that it seems impossible that the most famous of them all had still to be invented. But he had. And it is still more interesting that here, too, that character's most famous phrase didn't come out right first time. Who that character was, and what the phrase was, we shall be seeing soon.

By this time Tommy and the gang were estimated to be attracting some sixteen million listeners each week, although that can only be a guess since the sophisticated audience research methods of today had not yet evolved. How did this fame affect Tommy Handley? It was, after all, the biggest audience any regular radio show had ever attracted. The short answer seems to be that it changed him not at all. The weekly letters home to his mother were written as regularly as clockwork. He answered most of his mail himself, just a short one- or two-line note in most cases, but always in his own hand, snatching every spare second during rehearsals to get them done.

He lived as quietly as ever. Never one for the high life, he grabbed

B.B.C.
London
Dec 13/40

My dear Pam

Thank you for your nice
letter with snaps — Of course I remember
your Mummy and "Aunty Dot" will you
give them my love — I have returned the
Photo of the Concert Party as I already
have one and maybe Aunty Dot would
like to keep it — tell her I often think of
those happy days at Llandrindod Well —
I like your pictures I think you look very
Saucy as Buttons — perhaps some day you
will be in a real Pantomime. I hope so.
Now I must go and try to catch "Funf"
Love from Tommy Handley
J. T. M. A.

This is not *Funf speaking*

as much free time as he could with his wife, Jean, who had inevitably
had to be left behind during the Jack Hylton tours. He drank little,
but enjoyed the company of his fellows over a beer. He smoked his
pipe continually, but quite often with it empty. He was making a lot
58 of money by the standards of radio of those days: he was certainly

not wasting it. The old uncertainty, endemic in the profession, was still there. The audience might tire of you, and what then? The thrift he had learned in his Liverpool boyhood had not left him. Life can't go on being as good as this: there is bound to be a rainy day some time soon.

But there wasn't. What there was was the proudest day of Tommy's life. Early in March 1942, he was sitting in the studio going through his mail when one letter stopped him in his tracks. After an exclamation of disbelief, he handed the letter to Kavanagh to read:

WINDSOR CASTLE

2nd March, 1942.

PRIVATE AND CONFIDENTIAL

Tommy Handley Esq.,
c/o BBC.,
Bangor,
Caernarvonshire.
N. Wales.

DEAR SIR,
The King and Queen have expressed the desire to see a performance of your Company.

As you are in Wales, and not knowing what your professional engagements may be, I do not know whether it would be possible to arrange a performance at Windsor next month. An appropriate date would be about the 21st April, which is the Princess Elizabeth's birthday.

If this could be arranged without serious inconvenience to yourself and your company, I would suggest that if you have an Agent in London he might come down to Windsor Castle and see the hall which is used for such entertainments. I wish to stress that Their Majesties particularly desire that there should be no interference with any of your professional engagements.

Will you kindly treat this letter as strictly confidential.

Yours truly
(Signed) P. W. Legh.
Master of the Household.

I don't mind if you do!

8

IT WAS THE first ever Royal Command *Radio* Show, so everybody connected with the programme was bursting with pride. They were also filled with frustration, since they were under strict instructions not to say anything about the honour for security reasons: the news that on a certain day the entire Royal Family would be at Windsor Castle must not leak out. Tommy told his wife Jean but on this occasion felt that his weekly letter to his mother must leave out the one piece of news he would have been proudest to tell her.

But there were still four ordinary shows to be got through before the Royal, so they all took a deep breath and went back to the daily grind. Then came The Day. The entire cast travelled by train to Euston and then by coach to Windsor. As with any Royal occasion, there was a great deal of initial solemnity, with people talking in awed whispers. Until, that is, the door of the Castle buildings was opened by an official. 'Got any digs?' came the voice of Tommy Handley. The ice was broken and everybody visibly relaxed and went inside to start rehearsing. The event (which also included acts by Robb Wilton, Vera Lynn, Jack Warner, Kenway and Young, and Max Geldray, since the Royals had asked for a two-hour show) was a great success. The senior members of the cast were presented to the Royal Family, who revealed what great fans of the programme they were, and sent everybody away happy. Tommy went straight home to tell Jean about the day, and to settle down to write to his mother. And then back to Bangor for the rest of the series.

The summer break was very necessary. Tommy was working no harder than Worsley and Kavanagh, but they all knew the strain he was under in having to carry the show. It is doubtful whether all his lines put together ever added up to more than about ten or twelve minutes out of the half-hour programme, but he was at the centre of things for the whole time and everybody knew that, despite the immense talents of the rest of the cast, it all depended on him once that red transmission light went on. A short holiday with Jean and his mother was the only time off he could spare, but it was something. And the immense popularity of the show did ensure that the adrenalin kept pumping into the veins, making the strain just that little bit more bearable.

Tommy was now fifty and, although superficially as fit as any man of that age can be, he occasionally gave his doctor cause for alarm when he went for one of his regular check-ups. But how could the instructions to let up be obeyed? He knew, and Worsley and Kavanagh knew, just how important the programme was to national morale. 1942 was not a good war year for Britain and her allies. In the Far East it seemed that nothing could stop the Japanese. They'd taken Singapore, Rangoon, and Mandalay. Nothing seemed likely to prevent them sweeping up through Burma into India. In the Pacific, Corregidor and Bataan had surrendered. In Russia the Germans were still racing onwards, although there were signs of a Russian counter-offensive. In North Africa, Rommel took Tobruk and pushed the British further and further east towards the Nile. At home, after a temporary respite from German bombs, the so-called Baedeker raids were taking their toll of historic cities such as Bath and Exeter.

It was therefore essential that the *ITMA* team, no matter how tired it was feeling, should keep up the good work. The healing power of laughter was never more needed than during that year. So back the gang came in September 1942, for yet another series, the fifth in fact, with more than sixty shows already behind them. The setting was still Foaming-at-the-Mouth, but a munitions factory had been added to the place. Tommy, naturally, took on the job of running it, although it was never clear just what sort of munitions they made there. But then it was never clear what his duties as Mayor of the town involved either. Not that anybody cared, as long as Tommy and Co. made them laugh twice a week (once for the original transmission, once for the recorded Sunday evening repeat, which an enormous number of people listened to again). In fact, Tommy was making them laugh on more occasions than that, for the cast were continually doing concerts for those shift workers who never got a chance to hear either the original or the repeat. In view of the extreme difficulty of moving around wartime Britain, with railways damaged by bombings, roads unsignposted and unlit, and petrol rationed, how they managed to keep up the schedule for so long is a mystery. It took its toll of Jack Train, who was later to leave the cast for a year, during which time he was very seriously ill. But it equally took its toll of Tommy, though this was less immediately obvious. The hypertension which finally killed him wasn't helped in the slightest by the punishing schedules of those days.

But they were schedules that had to be adhered to if the *ITMA* team was to do its duty as it saw it. And it had every intention of doing so. New characters kept cropping up. Fred Yule added Norman the Doorman to his impressive list of impersonations, so 'Vicky verky' became another national saying. He also became that jovial German, Johann Bull, who would have his 'little choke'. Jack Train, who had played so many characters by now that he and everybody else had lost count, had added two more. The first was Mr Bookham the variety agent, who had come in just before the summer break. The second was that most famous of all his creations, Colonel Chinstrap. In fact, the Colonel had existed for some time before he actually said anything, as a result of constant references to him by Tommy. (The pace of production, and the sheer number of shows and characters, some of whom might exist for one week only, is probably the reason why, in his own book *ITMA*, Francis Worsley, who after all was the producer of the show, brings the Colonel into the programme exactly twelve months before he actually appeared on the scene!) In the very first dialogue the character was unidentified, but the style was unmistakable:

Tommy: *Didn't I meet you in Rumbellipore, sir?*
Voice: *You did not, sir. I was never there.*
Tommy: *Then you must have a double.*
Voice: *Thanks, I will.*

Once again, as in the case of Dorothy Summers' Mrs Mopp, the final line wasn't quite right. But once they stumbled on it, 'I don't mind if I do' entered into the language and, indeed, is still there, often delivered in the Colonel's fruity tones, over thirty years later.

This series ran from September 1942 through to January 1943, when there was another short break. But break is the wrong word for it. There were more shows to be given at halls throughout the country, especially in the industrial areas. *ITMA* may have been primarily a radio programme, in which much of the work was done by the listeners' imaginations, but people still wanted to see the team in action, and to see how much the characters corresponded to the mental pictures they had drawn of them. So the relentless grind went on. It felt less like a grind, of course, because the team worked so well together, and because they had so much fun. Nevertheless the strain

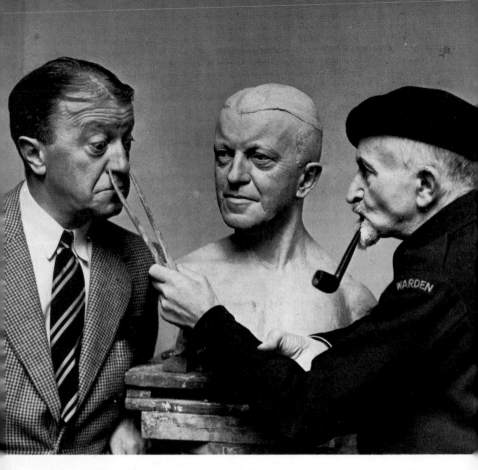

Immortality or bust. Sculptor Whitney Smith with his bust of Tommy for Madame Tussauds

continued to grow. To the public, everybody connected with *ITMA* seemed to be bursting with health and high spirits. But in fact Jack Train was a very sick man and becoming sicker, and it was about this time, too, that Fred Yule first became seriously concerned about Tommy's health and began a series of friendly warnings to him to take things a bit easier. The advice had to be highly informal, of course; just casually dropped into the conversation alongside a remark that he himself, Fred, was feeling a bit whacked. Tommy was undoubtedly king of the castle, but paranoia often goes hand in hand with monarchy. Any suggestion that they could do without him for a little while invariably put him on the defensive. The man who feels he is indis-

pensable often takes any hint that he isn't as the sign of a plot to remove him. But, as the French statesman Clemenceau used to point out, the cemeteries of the world are full of indispensable men. In the end, of course, Tommy Handley *was* indispensable. Without him there could have been no *ITMA*, which is why his death in January 1949 brought the show to an immediate end. But in January 1943, Tommy felt fit enough to laugh away any warnings he received.

Within a very short time the cast was re-assembling for another series. Their audience was now bigger than it had ever been, for since November 1942 it had been relayed by short wave to the troops in West Africa and to North Africa where Montgomery's men, after the victory over Rommel at El Alamein, were now chasing the German and Italian forces back across that dusty and much fought-over terrain. The church bells had rung out in Britain for the first time since the start of the war. The restriction had originally been to enable them to be used as a warning that the German invasion of this country had started. Now they were ringing out for victory. Prime Minister Winston Churchill described the events in North Africa as 'if not the beginning of the end, at least the end of the beginning'. But for the *ITMA* team the end was nowhere near, although they were not to know that then. The rewarding, but exhausting, slog was only one-third over. There were still six more years to go. If only they had had any means of knowing what the future had in store for them, some of them might have felt even more tired than they actually did.

Dug in at the dug out – Charles Shadwell with Handley and Kavanagh. Overleaf: Once more with feeling! Charles Shadwell conducts the orchestra and Messrs Percival, Yule, Wright and Handley

9

THE SUMMER SERIES of 1943, which ended on 5 August, went out with a bang, for that date produced the one hundredth show. It also saw the end of the Variety Department's long stay in long-suffering Bangor. In fact, Bangor saw them off with sadness. They may have been looked on as scarlet women and wicked men, strolling vagabonds and rogues to boot, when they first arrived in the little North Wales town in February 1941. By the time they left in the late summer of 1943 they were looked on as old friends. But the difficulties of organising variety programmes eight hours away from London—for that is what it took in those days—were becoming very great. Since it was clear to everybody that the worst of the air raids were over—they weren't, in fact: and the V1, or buzz bomb, and the V2 rocket were also waiting in the wings, but who could have guessed that?—the BBC took the undoubtedly correct decision to bring the entire Variety Department back to the capital.

As far as the *ITMA* cast were concerned, it was a lucky break, for they were given the Criterion Theatre, which the Corporation had taken over until the end of hostilities. Acoustically, it was perfect, as might have been expected. But in terms of character and comfort it was exactly right too. The stage was extended over the first four rows of the stalls, the stage box became the control cubicle, and since the audience was only allowed in the stalls area, the circle and balcony could be dormitories for firewatchers and those who could not get home through the black-out (which still existed). And all of the cast recognised immediately that the most intangible of all theatre qualities, its character, was absolutely *sympathique*.

As they prepared to open, Francis Worsley and Ted Kavanagh had to face up to one or two cast changes. Jack Train's illness now became too serious for him to continue. He was packed off to a sanatorium in North Wales, where he stayed for more than a year, and where that 67

seemingly infinite range of voices rested too, of course. As Worsley and Kavanagh thought characters like the Colonel were unique, they wisely decided to avoid any imitations. This threw an extra burden on the rest of the cast, which by now included Bill Stephens as Comical Chris. Horace Percival, creator of Ali Oop, the Diver, Cecil, and dozens of others, now added Mr What's'isname to his repertoire, the man who could never finish a sentence and whose original was a man Tommy Handley had met in London, or so Tommy swore. No one could ever tell whether on occasions like that he was being truthful or was just letting his imagination run riot.

Jean Capra, who joined the cast at this time, had the distinction, or ordeal, of being the first artist ever to be auditioned for the show. Until then Worsley had simply taken his actors from the tremendously versatile group of people called the Variety Rep, which had enormous advantages as long as the Department was in Bangor. But, now they were all back in London, it seemed only fair to try out new voices. Nerve-racking though auditions always are, Jean made an instant impression, and later became Poppy Poopah and lots of other characters. The old regulars were still there: Fred Yule, Dorothy Summers, Dino Galvani, Sydney Keith, Bill Stephens, Bryan Herbert, who had come from the BBC Drama Rep, and newcomer Jean. And, of course, there was Charles Shadwell, the thin conductor of the orchestra (though not as thin as Tommy implied when he called him 'A skewer with boots on' or something similar).

The locale of Tommy's adventures had changed a number of times over the years since Foaming-at-the-Mouth was first invented. But by the end of 1943 he had settled down in the country as the Squire of Much-Fiddling Manor. Then at the very end of the year came news of a totally different location. The Admiralty suggested that the *ITMA* team might like to go up to Scapa Flow and entertain the men and women of the Navy there, men and women who, by geography and the nature of their duties, were as cut off from home as if they had been officially overseas. On 6 January 1944, after they had finished the regular show, they all went home to pack, and met again the next morning at Euston where they caught the train to Thurso. There they embarked on board an ex-Swedish steamer for the last stage of their thirty-six-hour journey. Their reception was tremendous. They stayed in the Orkneys for five days, and in addition to doing a 'real' *ITMA* for ordinary transmission, they did *fifteen* one-and-a-half-hour shows before they were flown, exhausted, back to the mainland and so to London. And also to bed!

70   It was obvious, after the success of the naval *ITMA*, that there

At Scapa Flow

would have to be RAF and Army versions too. There were; the RAF one was held in February in the normal way in the Criterion and wasn't really a great success. London had too many other attractions for the programme to be as special as it was for those lonely matelots up in Scapa Flow. So the Army one, in April, was arranged for the Garrison Theatre at Woolwich, and went with a bang. But it should be remembered that each one of these services shows meant extra work for all the artists. New jokes, new phrases, had to be dug out and incorporated, specially appropriate musical arrangements had to be written for the orchestra: 'What shall we do with a drunken sailor?' for the Navy, 'Music while you Erk' for the RAF, and 'Colonel Bogey' for the Army. It all added up to yet more strain for the hard-working team. It is no wonder that producer Francis Worsley began to feel the effects, and was soon, like Jack Train, to have to go into hospital for a long period.

Home cooking – Tommy and Jean

It made them laugh too! Dorothy Summers, Bryan Herbert and Paula Green with Tommy and Ted

But for all the worried glances of the older members of the team, Tommy and Ted Kavanagh, on whom the greatest strain naturally fell, seemed to be bearing up very well. Wherever they went they seemed to be on top of their form. All the programmes, of course, were not successes. A show from the Wolseley factory near Birmingham, then making tanks, was an undoubted flop, probably because it was the first show of the new season which started in September, and because munition workers, going home at the end of their shifts, obviously did not have the same unified sense of identity as the Forces. Tommy, sensitive as usual to criticism, was severely shaken by some of the unkind remarks which the Wolseley broadcast drew.

But there were one or two cheering things as well. Jack Train, now recovered after his year in a sanatorium, was back with the show, inevitably bringing the Colonel with him. And because Paula Green, one of the singers who had been with *ITMA* for ages, had gone off on an overseas ENSA tour, a replacement had been brought in. In fact, she wasn't a singer, but she was to prove one of the most memorable characters of the ten years of *ITMA*'s life. Diana Morrison had actually joined the team towards the end of the previous series, but in the second of the new September 1944 shows a stern, commanding voice rang out for the first time: 'MR HANDLEY!' Miss Hotchkiss, that most domineering of all secretaries, had arrived. From then on Mrs Handley's boy was never to have a moment of peace, even though he seemed to have become some sort of Minister of Reconstruction (D-Day was already far behind and the war looked as though it would soon come to an end). His Ministry appeared to consist very largely of talking about his Plan although, in true *ITMA* tradition, it was never made clear just what was in the Plan or what it was that was going to be Planned.

With Miss Hotchkiss, the programme took on yet another lease of life. From her very first appearance, she became a household name. And by this time it would have been correct to add 'throughout the world'. *ITMA* was now going out on Thursdays on the Home Service, on Sundays on the General Forces Programme, on Mondays on the Pacific Service, on Wednesdays on the General Forces again, on Wednesday nights on the General Overseas Service, and on Tuesday mornings on the North American Service. When the African Service was added a little later, Tommy Handley was surely working to a bigger audience, covering a bigger part of the earth's surface, than anyone had ever done before. It was during this series that Jack Train introduced yet another catchphrase, from the lips of an incredibly ancient-sounding gentleman, Mark Time, who, despite his vast age,

replied to every question by saying 'I'll have to ask me Dad'. Some months later, during the 1945 General Election, Randolph Churchill, the son of the Prime Minister, was asked a question on the hustings. Before he could answer, a heckler cut in with 'I'll have to ask me Dad'.

At the turn of the year, Francis Worsley found that the lumbago he had been troubled with for some time was, in fact, something far worse, and off he went to hospital. But the *ITMA* routine was so set now— Tommy, Francis and Ted Kavanagh working for three solid days on Ted's first draft—that Francis's hospital ward became the programme's HQ. Francis produced the show from his bed, and Ronnie Waldman, that splendid BBC stalwart, took over on the studio floor. It was perhaps inevitable that within weeks Tommy was in charge of 'Tommy's Hospital'. Since Mrs Mopp was the Matron, it was clearly an institution being run with the usual *ITMA* efficiency.

By now it was obvious to all except those Germans surrounding Hitler that the war in Europe was coming to an end. The Luftwaffe was in no position to attack Britain any more, and the V1 and V2 bases had been over-run by the Allies, so the threat of disruption by aerial attack was quite definitely over. London had an air of expectancy about it. Black-out restrictions had been successively relaxed over the past months and everybody was planning what they were going to do 'when the lights come on again all over the world'. The *ITMA* team was amongst them: a special edition would be required. Happily, Francis Worsley was well enough to be allowed out of hospital and so resumed command just in time to prepare the show. It was broadcast on Thursday, 10 May, between 8.30 and 9.00 pm, ten days after Hitler committed suicide in his Berlin bunker, and just two days after the official VE-Day declaration. The first great *ITMA* period was over, a period in which the varying, but somehow strangely constant-sounding, *ITMA* team in general, and Tommy Handley in particular, had helped the nation to keep sane during some of the darkest and most testing days it had ever been called on to face during its history. Tommy's voice had always seemed to prove that whatever happened, we wouldn't go under. Of course that remark, on the face of it, is vastly over-stated: if the Germans had invaded this country immediately after Dunkirk, no radio comic could have had the slightest effect on the outcome. But the Germans didn't invade us. Britain was therefore stuck with a long, weary, dreary stretch, in which we seemed, certainly in Europe, to be involved in precious little fighting, except to be on the receiving end of what there was. Because of the lack of inspiration in such a period, morale could have become very low. At times, in fact, it did; but it is certain that it would have been very much lower if it hadn't been for our weekly injection of the sort of confidence Mrs Handley's boy exuded, and never once stopped exuding, through all those difficult years. They may have been the British people's finest hours. They were also Tommy Handley's.

10

THAT VICTORY *ITMA* was the 172nd programme in the series. As the first four were transmitted during the last month before the war started that means that no fewer than 168 had been wartime issues. It seemed obvious to some people—outside the BBC as well as inside—that the end of the war in Europe, or at any rate the end of the war in the Pacific, would see the end of the useful role everyone agreed the programme had played throughout the hostilities. Even so, this meant the show might continue for some considerable time, as the Pacific War was generally expected to be bloody and long-lasting: nobody, of course, with the exception of a tiny handful of scientists, knew about the atom bomb.

Its use on Hiroshima and Nagasaki brought that war to a stupefyingly sudden close. But by this time, the post-VE-Day honeymoon had ended. People had begun to realise that, far from all our troubles disappearing 'when they sang the last all clear', they were, in fact, only just beginning. Yet another tough time lay ahead of us. And the *ITMA* gang therefore found themselves, without any conscious decision on anybody's part, carrying on as before. There may not have been an enemy outside the gates to make fun of, but there were many within. Bureaucracy did not wither away with the end of war. Rather, it seemed to increase. But how to poke fun at it without running into political difficulties? Shortages and infuriating rules and regulations could, in the past, always be laid, however indirectly, at Hitler's door. Now they could very easily be seen to be laid at the door of Britain's first-ever majority Labour Government.

The solution was one which had been thought of before—by Jonathan Swift, among others. Shift the scene to some far-away

Opposite: Mr Handley! *Miss Hotchkiss (Diana Morrison) interrupts the Governor introducing Ella Phant (Hattie Jacques) to the delights of work*

B. B. C.

London 9/3/46

Dear Mr Procter

Thank you for sending suggested idea for "Itma" - it is very good but just at the moment I am governing Tomtopia ?! and am likely to do so until the present series finishes - Perhaps when I resume in Sept you will send it in again.

my best wishes.

Tommy Handley

island, satirise its institutions, and let people in this country see if the cap fitted at home as well as abroad. Which is why a recently discovered island, a tropical paradise called Tomtopia, was invented. And who but Tommy Handley could be its Governor?

The idea was that the first programme of the new post-summer series would reveal Tommy's promotion. There would then be a couple of programmes about the preparations, followed by a four-week sea voyage as the characters journeyed to the island (some old hands doubtless remembered that the first *ITMA* series, exactly six years earlier, had started with a four-week sea voyage). The change of location was a help in another way, because important cast changes had become necessary. Dorothy Summers, Sydney Keith, Dino Galvani, and Horace Percival all left, a formidable loss. Jack Train, Fred Yule, Diana Morrison and Jean Capra stayed on, but it was obvious that reinforcements were needed. Clarence Wright returned after his stage tour, and was joined by Hugh Morton, Mary O'Farrell, Carleton Hobbs, and Lind Joyce, who was the team's singer as well as having a very useful range of non-singing voices.

Their presence meant a new set of characters, all as mad as their predecessors, and a new set of catchphrases. Hugh Morton's Sam Fairfechan was a Welshman who spoke his more offensive thoughts aloud: 'Good morning and how are you? *As if I cared*!' Fred Yule produced possibly his best remembered role, and catchphrase; as George Gorge, the greediest man in the world, the relish with which he said 'luvly grub' made a nation still using ration books laugh with distinctly watering mouths.

It took six weeks for Tommy to get his cast to the island of Tomtopia and no time at all for him to settle in as Governor, helped by the able Miss Hotchkiss, who only arrived in the nick of time; Diana Morrison had in fact been ill for the six weeks the voyage was supposed to have taken. The Governor was soon on good terms with the native chief, Bigga Banga, another Fred Yule creation, whose unintelligible gibberish, called Utopi in the script, was delightfully translated for us by Lind Joyce as his daughter Banjolele, who started every explanation with the words 'My Papa he say . . .'

Charles Shadwell, whom Tommy had insulted for his thinness in just about every programme since 1941, now took himself off on tour with his orchestra. His place as conductor was taken by Rae Jenkins, who very soon became a butt of another kind, since he showed himself constitutionally incapable of ever reading any line correctly. Characters like Ruby Rockcake (Mary O'Farrell), with her British Railways' bellow of 'Noa cups outside', made it quite clear that though Tom-

Lead me away from temptation (in the shape of Molly Weir and Lind Joyce)

topia might be a far-away paradise it bore a remarkable similarity to another island situated just off the northwest coast of Europe. The Swiftian device was working. Newspapers fell into the habit of referring to Tommy as 'The Governor' as though Tomtopia was a real place. But we all knew the island's true name was Britain, and how much more fun it would have been had it been run the way Tomtopia was, rather than in the drab, austere, rationed way it had to be in the restricting aftermath of the war. But, as real-life circumstances changed, so too must *ITMA*, if it was to reflect, as it always had done, life as it was being lived. When the end of the series came along in April 1946 Tommy Handley said goodbye to the island and sailed back to see what the Old Country was going to get up to next.

But it wasn't goodbye. It was merely *au revoir*. The beginning of the next series, in the autumn of 1946, saw Tommy Handley back on his right little, tight little (well, Colonel Chinstrap was there) island. It also saw further examples of the way the programme, through the years, was able to come up with new characters when all ordinary

You buy pretty post card . . . very saucy . . . . very warm

On film with Ali Oop. Very chummy, oh lumme!

people must have thought the well had long since run dry. The most notable of this new batch of creations was that quintessential Scouse, Frisby Dyke. This was Deryck Guyler's first venture into light entertainment—he had primarily been a straight actor—and it is a measure of the impact he made on the public that even today people who claim to have been devout *ITMA* fans refuse to believe that he didn't first appear very much earlier than the 1947 series. Frisby's catchphrase—if indeed it was that—was his habit of popping up just after Tommy had used some complicated word, and asking what it meant. As a recipe for humour it sounds a non-starter, but in practice it used to stop the show. For example, after an orchestral piece:

> Tommy: *Rae, never in the whole of my three hundred* ITMA*s have I heard such a piece of concentrated cacophony.*
> Frisby: *What's concentrated cacophony?*

delivered, of course, in Deryck Guyler's own special, thickly adenoidal, 81

ITMA *takes to the road: in England and,* below, *Francis, Tommy and* Ted *set sail for the U.S.A.*

Scouse accent, an accent which Tommy, since he was born with it, could do to perfection but hadn't used for years. Later in the programme Frisby would get his own back, throwing the phrase—which had never been explained—straight back at Handley in a different context.

Another new character whose accent could instantly be imitated was Molly Weir's Tattie Macintosh; so was massive Hattie Jacques' tiny-voiced greedy schoolgirl, Sophie Tuckshop. As it turned out, Hattie achieved one distinction she never wanted. She was the last artist to join the *ITMA* team, for, as the reference to 'three hundred Itmas' above shows, the end was near. In the various series since the return of Tomtopia in the autumn of 1946, *ITMA* had sent a rocket to the moon—and missed, naturally; Tommy had become the Government's scientific adviser, with catastrophic results, but perhaps no more catastrophic than what was happening in the real world outside; and he had also gone down in the world, becoming a permanent resident of a tramps' home, delightfully named Henry Hall. But despite all the changes of locale and plot(!), or perhaps because of them, the show never showed any signs of flagging. The humour was as mad, and as therapeutic, as ever. There seemed to be no way in which it could ever stop. But appearances, as usual, were deceptive.

Tommy's health was now beginning to break up under the strain. It wasn't just the programmes. It was the other things that *ITMA* almost necessarily brought with it; appearances here, performances there, openings in one place, beauty queen judgings in another. Nor was it possible to refuse them. Radio in those days was still the chief form of home entertainment. Just as with TV today, so with radio then: those who appeared on it were people whom we regularly welcomed into our homes. They were our friends. We wanted to see them, to shake them by the hand. And they saw it as their duty—giving back something to the public which had given them so much—to go out of their way to make it possible for us to meet them.

The round of engagements never ended. Wherever he went, Tommy was his usual bright, bubbling, extrovert self, making people laugh, and apparently enjoying every second of it. But he wasn't. Photographs of that time show him as elegant and jaunty as ever; good quality overcoat, elegant scarf, trilby hat cocked at just the right angle, and always that friendly smile. But a closer examination of them shows something else. Lines of strain; a drawn quality; the face of a man who is deadly tired but whose job requires him, as clowns have always been required, to put a face on, a face which may bear no relation whatsoever to what the clown is feeling or thinking.

Handley and Kenneth Horne share a bottle of wine while, below, there's beer for the boys.

Facing page, the 300th ITMA. Left to right Tommy, Lind Joyce, Clarence Wright, Dorothy Summers, Deryck Guyler, Fred Yule and Jack Train

So it was with Tommy. More and more, Fred Yule and the other
old-stagers urged Tommy to ease up. More and more they urged him
not to take so much notice of whatever bad reviews the show—
inevitably—sometimes got. But it was no use. The old insecurity, the
old sensitivity, drove him on, and while driving him on, left him wide
open to all sorts of assaults, both mental and physical, on his tired
frame.

The three hundredth performance had been honoured by the
presence in the audience of Princess Margaret, who, with her mother
and father, had also visited the show on the occasion of the BBC's
Silver Jubilee during the '47/8 series. The programme was now in
its tenth year and showed every sign of being able to run for another
ten years. In fact, it ran for only ten more shows. Tommy was not
well. His hypertension was more menacing than ever. He still turned
up, punctual as usual, for all rehearsals and recordings, and his
performance was seldom below its usual staggeringly high level. But
some critics had begun to think that ten years was perhaps too much of
a good thing, and that maybe the show should be taken off for ever.
And having thought that, it was in the nature of those critics to start
panning the programme.

Fred Yule is convinced it was this that, in the end, really killed

Tommy Handley. It is doubtful. His assessment is almost certainly that of a man who loved Tommy, was shattered by his death, and looked desperately, but understandably, around for someone to blame. But it is true that Jonah Barrington's criticisms in particular hurt Tommy deeply. Fred and Tommy had long been in the habit of lunching at the Savage Club on the day after each *ITMA* broadcast. He recalled that Tommy would refuse to eat until he had read what the critics had to say. And if the reviews were bad he would have no appetite, despite Fred's urgings. 'Why not eat first, and read them afterwards?' he would say. But Tommy wouldn't be budged. The papers would be opened with trembling hands, the eyes would race down the column, that most jaunty of faces would sag, and he would suddenly look very, very old.

The end came on 9 January 1949. The 310th show had gone out, as usual, on the Thursday evening, to be repeated, as a recording, on the following Sunday. Leaving the Paris Cinema, where the programme had been put on ever since the Criterion had returned to its rightful job of putting on live theatre, Tommy was tired, but in good spirits, and looking forward to a weekend's rest. On the Sunday he wakened up with a severe headache, but decided that, rather than go back to bed, or mope indoors, he would dress and go out for some fresh air. While dressing, he dropped his collar stud. He bent down to pick it up, and was instantly struck with a massive cerebral haemorrhage. His wife Jean, only recently returned from hospital herself, struggled to bring him round, but he was completely unconscious. The doctor was sent for, and Tommy was whipped off to a nursing home where he underwent a lumbar puncture, but it was too late. Britain's best-loved broadcaster was dead.

At 5.30 that Sunday evening the 310th *ITMA* went out as a repeat as usual. It ended, there was a short silence, and then a stunned nation heard the reader of the six o'clock news start the bulletin with the words: 'The BBC regrets to announce the death of Mr Thomas Handley, the comedian.'

It was unbelievable. The man we had been laughing at only a moment before was dead. That Man, who had been with us so long, and through so many hard times, would be with us no more.

EPILOGUE

THE CROWDS OUTSIDE the chapel in Westbourne Grove were enormous. All along the route of the procession people lined the pavements, the men with their heads bare, many of the women weeping. At the Golders Green crematorium the crowds were so vast they were almost uncontrollable. In the chapel the organ played, the coffin slid forward into the furnace, and a group of Tommy's Brother Savages sang Sullivan's 'The Long Day Closes' as it has surely never been sung before or since—Trefor Jones, Parry Jones, Walter Midgley, Webster Booth, Dennis Noble, Frederick Gregory, George James, and Edward Dykes—all great artists and all of them moved to tears by the passing of one of their dearest friends.

Twelve days later there was a memorial service in St Paul's Cathedral. More than two thousand people stood bareheaded in the churchyard. Inside, four thousand listened to John Snagge, a famous BBC voice, read from Ecclesiasticus the lines beginning 'Let us now praise famous men'. The choir, augmented by the women as well as the men of the BBC singers (the first time women had ever sung from those choirstalls), sang extracts from the Brahms 'Requiem', and Sir Walford Davies' beautifully simple setting of 'God be in my head'. The prayers were led by the Dean of St Paul's, Dr W. R. Matthews; and the Bishop of London, the Right Reverend J. W. C. Wand, in his address, summed up Tommy Handley's achievement in words which cannot be beaten for truth and beauty:

'His genius transmuted the copper of our common experience into the gold of exquisite foolery. His raillery was without cynicism and his satire without malice. Who could tell how great a benefit he conferred upon the nation in the days of its grimmest endeavour, as he brought week by week to millions an overflowing measure of irresistible laughter and the iridescent froth and bubble of the professional jester? From the highest to the lowest in the land people had found in his programme an escape from their troubles and anxieties into a world of whimsical nonsense.'

The memorial service at Liverpool Cathedral was in no sense an anti-climax: indeed the crowds attending the service were the greatest ever known there. And why not? This was Tommy's hometown. This was where he was born and brought up, this was where he acquired that absolutely inimitable Liverpudlian sense of humour, the resilience that was his own special trademark. The crowds were as shaken and as silent as they had been in London as they listened to the Rev. Eric Evans take as his text: 'God hath made me to laugh, so that all who hear will laugh with me.' His sermon was particularly fitted to the occasion, with the sound of the ships' hooters drifting up from the Mersey: 'I speak for many who during the war went down to the sea in ships. I was one of them, and can testify from personal experience to the welcome relief the weekly broadcasts of *ITMA* brought to us. Tommy Handley was unique in the realm of broadcasting, and he won a place of affection in every rank of society. He was in every sense a true jester.' Liverpool had lost its most famous citizen and Liverpool, a hard town with a great warm heart, was mourning him.

Yet in a way it was all most inappropriate. Tommy had been our court jester for so long that it might have been more fitting had the farewells been less sad. Ted Kavanagh wrote in his biography of Tommy that he could imagine him looking down at it all—at Golders Green, at St Paul's, at Liverpool, and saying 'Gosh, this can't all be for me? There must be some mistake. I should be rehearsing *ITMA* today.'

I'm sure he was right. But I'm even more sure that the modest, and doubtless slightly embarrassed, pleasure he'd have derived from the various tributes would have been as nothing compared with his joy at learning that the man who conducted the cremation service at Golders Green, the Rev. J. F. Macdonald, later confessed,' I suppose I am the only man in the country who has never ever listened to an *ITMA* broadcast.'

Tommy would have loved that. Always a connoisseur of life's little ironies, that particular twist would surely have pleased him greatly. I can see him throw his head back with laughter as he says, 'Well, I'll jump off the end of the pier with a jam butty in each hand! TTFN!' The sad thing is that it wasn't 'Ta ta for now!' It was TTFE. Ta ta for evermore.

"TOMMY" BY LESLIE ILLINGWORTH
10 JAN 1949

Acknowledgements

I am enormously indebted to all the people who took the trouble to reply to my letters in the papers asking for help, and who sent me letters, photographs and cherished mementoes. Among these, special thanks go to Anne Benson, Celia Michaelides, Stella Pitchford and Harry Williams. I am also indebted to Tommy's (and my) Brother Savages, particularly the Hon. Sec. Alan Wykes and the Club's irreplaceable secretary, Mrs Dora Phillips.

I would like to thank Mrs Agnes Kavanagh for her kind permission to include extracts from *ITMA*, and the BBC for the inclusion of Murgatroyd and Winterbottom material.

Acknowledgement is also due to the following organisations for their permission to reproduce illustrations: BBC copyright (pp. 8, 28, 30–1, 41, 72, 80); Bradford *Telegraph & Argus* (p. 42); Ronald Grant Collection (pp. 32, 81); Hodder and Stoughton Ltd (pp. 11, 14, 18, 24, 33, 54 —from *Tommy Handley* by Ted Kavanagh); Keystone Press Agency (pp. 60, 72); Mander and Mitchenson Theatre Collection (pp. 26, 47); Pathé Film Library (pp. 36, 39); Popperfoto (pp. 44, 48–9, 52, 64, 66, 68–9, 76, 82, 84, 85); The Press Association (pp. 84, 88); Radio Times Hulton Picture Library (p. 6); Universal Pictorial Press & Agency Ltd (p. 87).

Index

Allistone, Jean, 32-3, 58, 61, 86; marriage to Tommy Handley, 32

Askey, Arthur, 9

Barrington, Jonah, 86; criticisms of Tommy Handley, 86

Bennett, Billy, 9

Bennett and Williams, 37

Benson, Anne, 12, 13

Blore, Eric, 23

Booth, Webster, 89

Brewer, Charles, 40

British Broadcasting Corporation: failure of idea to create stardom for Tommy Handley, 40, 43; moves to Bristol, 46; further move from Bristol to Bangor, 54; return to London, 67

Burns and Allen, 40, 43

Capra, Jean, 70, 79

Champion, Harry, 43

Churchill, Randolph, 74

Churchill, Sir Winston, 65

Clapham & Dwyer, 37

Coburn, Charles, 43

Costa, Sam, 47, 56

Cottrell, Sam, 19

Denham, Maurice, 47, 50, 53, 56

Diamond, Rex, 34

'Disorderly Room, The', 23-5, 54

Dodd, Ken, 9

Dykes, Edward, 89

Eddy, Celia, 45

Egan, Eric, 45

Elliott, G. H., 16-17

Frankau, Ronald, 35; as Murgatroyd in act with Tommy Handley, 35, 37-9

Galvani, Dino, 56, 70, 79

Geldray, Max, 61

Green, Paula, 73

Gregory, Frederick, 89

Guyler, Deryck, 81, 83

Haley, Sir William, 5

Handley, John (father), 9, 10

Handley, Sarah Anne (mother), 9, 12

Handley, Tommy: as man of the people, 5-6; death, 7, 86; birth, 9; poverty-stricken upbringing of, 9-10; possesses fine singing voice, 10; first stage appearance, 10-11; takes up ventriloquism, 11; in play, *A Bundle of Sticks*, 11; leaves school, 12; first job, 13; acting roles played, 13; appears in grand opera, 15; delayed call-up in First World War, 16; in *Maid of the Mountains*, 16; in Royal

93

Handley, Tommy:—*cont.*

Naval Air Service, 16; joins concert party, 16–17; friendship with Jack Hylton, 17; offered second comic job, 17; as lead comic in *Seasoned to Taste*, 18–19; in film, *The Laundry Girl*, 19; in *The Sparklers* concert party, 19–20; appearance and personality, 21; in sketch, 'The Disorderly Room', 23–5, 29, 32, 43; as lead comic in *Dancing Time*, 25; in revue, *The Whirl of the World*, 25; successful audition for BBC, 27, 29; in *Radio Radiance*, 32; meets Jean Allistone, 32; marriage to Jean Allistone, 32; his increasing radio fame, 33; thrift exercised by, 33–4, 58–9; in *Handley's Half Hour*, 34, 40; teams up with Ronald Frankau in Murgatroyd & Winterbottom act, 35; tours music halls, 43; does newspaper advertisements, 43; leaves for Bristol on outbreak of Second World War, 46; becomes a star with *ITMA*, 51; invited to appear at Royal Command Radio Show, 59, 61; industriousness of, 61–2; under intense stress and strain, 62–3; advice given to take things easier, 64–5, 85; universal success of, 75; break up of health, 83, 85; funeral, 89; tributes to, 89–90; memorial services, 89–90

Harris, Jack, orchestra of, 45
Harvey, Charles, 17
Henson, Leslie, 19, 23
Herbert, Bryan, 70
Hitler, Adolf, 29, 45, 75, 77
Hobbs, Carleton, 79
Howes, Bobby, 18, 19–20
Hylton, Jackson (Jack), 17, 47, 53; suggests partnership to Tommy Handley, 17–18; mounts stage version of *ITMA*, 53

ITMA (It's That Man Again), 7, 13, 16, 35, 45–7, 50–1, 53, 55, 62–3, 67, 70, 73–4, 79–83, 90; birth of, 43; first show, 45; characters in, 50–1, 56, 63, 73–4, 79, 81–3; size of listening audience, 56, 65, 73; Royal Command Show, 59–61; entertains Forces in Orkneys and London, 70–1; non-success at Wolseley factory, 73; Victory programme, 77

Jacques, Hattie, 83
James, George, 89
Jenkins, Rae, 79
Jewell, Jimmy, Sr, 25
Jones, Parry, 89
Jones, Trefor, 89
Joyce, Lind, 79

Kavanagh, Ted, 10, 33, 43, 46–7, 55, 56, 59, 67, 70, 73, 74
Kay, Gordon, 33
Keith, Sydney, 56, 70, 79
Kelly, Will, 12, 13
Kenway & Young, 61

Lennox, Vera, 47, 50, 56
Lester, Jimmy, 27
Lynn, Vera, 61

Macdonald, Rev. J. F., 90
Macpherson, Sandy, 46
Margaret, HRH Princess, 85
Maschwitz, Eric, 40
Matthews, Dr W. R., 89
Melford, Austin, 23
Mellor, Madame, 19
Merson, Billy, 25
Midgley, Walter, 89
Modley, Albert, 9
Morecambe & Wise, 21
Morrison, Diana, 73, 79
Morton, Hugh, 79
Murgatroyd & Winterbottom, extracts from act, 37–9